ॐ

OM N

SHI

AM 1ST

@ 11.15

CONVERSATIONS WITH MAHAVATAR BABAJI

MASTER PALLAVI

—

Illustrated by Jaspreet Matharu

First published in India in 2019

ISBN : 978-93-88333-74-0

Invincible Publishers

Registered Address: 201A, SAS Tower, Sector 38,
Gurgaon-122003

Printed at Replika Press Pvt. Ltd.

"We are Gods and we can converse with other gods. All is possible only through an intense Sadhana of Meditation. Anapanasati Meditation is the way of revolution for everyone. When the mind is clear, ATMA reveals itself to ATMA."

"Pallavi is our senior pyramid master. I am very glad she has experience with Mahavatar Babaji. Time has come for earth people to unite with extra-terrestrial."

"Be a vegetarian and be a meditator. Let us enjoy the essence of harmony in the Light Age."

Brahmarshi Pithamaha Patriji

INTRODUCTION

Mahavatar Babaji's work began with me at three different levels — Clairvoyance (I see), Clairaudience (I hear) and Clairsentience (I sense). It is indescribable what it feels like, however, I would describe it akin to receiving an e-mail, watching a video, picking up a phone call.. all at the same time and giving my best to interpret all three mediums in the limited human dictionary of words. If at all I could use words to describe this work, I would rather tell you, I was mostly at a loss of words experiencing the beyond while I was writing this book; however, it was a beautiful, adventurous and an ultimate experience on 'soul' level.

Working with Babaji meant getting messages in different styles of delivery, at times my body felt both light and heavy in vibration. I bow down to Him for the extraordinary awareness. He helped me to understand my exact state of mind and the way He triggered it, broke my shell of ignorance. This is a book which cannot be measured by its word count but rather by the level of energies shared and received in this work. Some days, I could write many pages.. and on other days, I could only manage a few paragraphs.

As long as I remember, as a child, I was very intuitive, born with psychic abilities by the grace of divine planning and my soul's blueprint. I conversed with my guardian angels and astral masters. As I grew up, I got entangled in this chaotic material world which filled my mind with doubts and questions.

I was able to converse with departed souls. They shared messages with me, which they wanted to give to the world or to a particular person. However, I was unaware and unsure on how to proceed by helping such souls. Going through these experiences, I had understood with absolute clarity, "Soul Never Dies". After I realized this truth, I never cried for anyone who have vacated their human body, not even my close family members. When I was in 12th standard, I had a classmate who sat in the row adjacent to me. She was an introvert, but we still spoke on a daily basis.

One day during my astral travel (out of body experience during sleep or what we know as dreams), I observed, she commited suicide and hung herself to death. I was just observing the whole scene. Exactly a week after my astral experience, I got news that she had committed suicide. This did not surprise me. Without reacting to the situation I traveled deep into my thoughts to see how I could really help such souls. I can now understand the suffering the soul went through. I was not carried away by the way people felt sympathetic towards them, but a deep level of understanding and empathy rose within me, which made me resilient in my decision to work for these souls. Many people are born with such psychic abilities.. but they do not know the science behind it. They in turn get into the job of making predictions and interfering with the experiences at individual level. These arises from their ignorance and they miss the opportunity of knowing the infinite possibilities of the Cosmos. You might not be aware initially of your entire journey in this lifetime, but you would discover them layer by layer, in a manner that you evolve holistically. This insures a right pattern of understanding of your PATH.

When people asked me if I knew Babaji, I always answered "NO" until I had a first-hand experience with His energies. As you expand your consciousness and awareness, you get to know the divine masters in bits and pieces through self-experience. I have come across many spiritual teachers of the spirit-world and knowing about their transformational stories gives me utmost enjoyment as well as uplifts my mind and soul. My passion to work with the spirit-world is increasing every day and I thoroughly enjoy diving deep within to research more about the beyond.

"Conversations with Mahavatar Babaji" is an effort through which you can develop an understanding of how super-conscious entities like Mahavatar Babaji work in different mediums and forms. Many of the subjects will seem strange to people, who haven't yet begun their journey on the Path of Spirituality, but it is an opportunity to let that energy start working within you at a sub-conscious level. This book is like a handbook or a spiritual start-up kit to take the first step towards an inner transformation and to feel Babaji's energies. Individuals familiar with Babaji Consciousness will enjoy every word of this book and will be thrilled to know more about his human life.

In the process of reading this book you will see how your understanding develops. As you read "Conversations With Mahavatar Babaji" certain fundamental mysterious facts of life will enable you to know and understand yourself better. This book will help all psychic minds, especially the ones already touched by the experience of Babaji in their life but seek more clarity or progress. This book is the first step in the direction of an unconditional understanding of walking into the unknown, as if it is known. The very consciousness of this book will make you feel, like you are holding your soul in a gentle but firm embrace, which is unfolding and enriching your life with a newer perspective. The special purpose of this book is to clarify to all believers and non-believers alike, how a physically immortal being like Mahavatar Babaji exists even in today's modern world; if receptive in absorbing the wisdom of Babaji's teachings it will help the seeker in the process of self-realization.

This journey with Babaji helped me personally, to know him as a "Universal Grand Soul" who is working in multiple ways with many people. I feel blessed and thankful that he chose me to record a part of his life-journey in this book. When my Soul Work began with Babaji He was unknown to me, but getting to know Him in this conscious physical reality was genuinely a beautiful surprise gift. I can still remember my first hazy encounter of His energies when I met with a bus accident. I could see with my open eyes three divine entities who saved me; one with long hair, one with a long beard and another one with a bald head. They were none other than Mahavatar Babaji, Brahmarshi Patriji and Lobsang Rampa who had come to my rescue! It was only after becoming a part of Pyramid Spiritual Societies Movement that I got to know about them, it was then the realization dawned upon me that the life of a spiritual person is always involved in the opening of the deep layers of life's mysteries.

ACKNOWLEDGMENTS

I bow down to my beloved Guru Brahmarshi Pithamaha Patriji for everything, especially for his valuable time and energy to edit this book and to my mentor, Mrs. Varalakshmi for being a storehouse of immense knowledge and a true guide.

My generous appreciation for Mr. Jaspreet Matharu for the soulful illustrations, which are absolutely awe-worthy and inspiring in many ways, and Mrs Prisila N Matharu for looking after our beloved book through the last stages of printing and publishing. I would also like to express my gratitude for their home that became an abode to the energies of Babaji's cave and my haven to get into the flow of writing easily.

I am deeply grateful to Mrs Radhika Mehrotra Taunk for playing the crucial role of editing this book and perfectly synchronizing my thoughts into words. Her love for Babaji made her a perfect choice to shape this book.

Extending my heartfelt gratitude to Mrs Charu T Vashistha, Ms Amita Pishen and Mr Deepak Agte for their strong faith in me and their valuable suggestions from time to time which helped to shape this book. I also appreciate all the advice which I received from everyone who have read the manuscript in its various stages of completion, including Mr Rajesh Khele, S. K. Rajan, Bottu Krishna Sathya, G. Rajashekhar, Aakash Suri, Shalini and Shravya.

Token recognition and thanks to my laptop that it was a gift, which made it so easy to compile my thoughts into a book. Finally, I salute and thank the indescribable energy force of Mahavatar Babaji, for being my true guiding light to be able to write His life-story.

PROLOGUE

"Babaji" is a familiar term in the Indian tradition, especially for those who have begun their journey on the path of spirituality.

My journey with Mahavatar Babaji began in the year 2009, when an awareness of love, divine aura and enchanting force behind this mystical name was created within me. The life-path for me since then has been memorable beyond imagination.

Born on September 3rd, 1986 in a classic traditional Hindu family in Beed District of Maharashtra, India —

I was handed down the legacy of 'God Praising' through rituals and mantras, typical in most Indian households. As a child, I worshiped God but neither could connect to the 'external propaganda' about God nor could find anyone who would answer my queries related to "God", especially the meaning behind the name.

Later, as a teenager, the quest to know the truth became deeper. I experienced subversive thoughts, which most of us go through to find God or the supreme reality. Finally, the day arrived in my life and my waiting to find the door, that would lead me to the light, was over.

It was when I was pursuing my graduation from Chennai, Tamil Nadu; my roommate's mother, a spiritual seeker taught me how to meditate. Initially, I was not so serious to follow it, neither try very hard.. but after four months, I felt a deep desire to meditate and hoped it would lead to the answers to all my questions about life beyond the ordinary existence.

It was midnight of April 22, 2006. I sat in meditation by closing my eyes, clasping my hands, crossing my legs and observed my natural breath. While observing my breathing pattern, I realized a basic truth about my mind — "I speak too much in my head and this needs to tone down". A thought struck me at that moment, how can we experience or see God with the non-stop churning of thoughts in our minds? I deeply felt that I needed to work on my thoughts and set myself free of negative patterns. I slowly came back to observing my breath.

15 minutes into the process, I could feel my mind becoming emptier and there was a great serenity within me for the first time. During the last two minutes of meditation, I saw a bright light illuminating within me; glowing bright like the sun. Surprised, I opened my eyes to see the source of this bright light, however, there was total darkness in the room. I closed my eyes again and saw the same light radiating from my body. My mind mumbled, "What is this light?" and I heard a voice that said, "Am your Atma (Soul)."

This was a life-changing experience of self-realization. There was no looking back and I became thirsty to know more, to be wiser and meditated intensively every day.

I had been practicing meditation for two months, when I got an opportunity to meet Brahmarshi Pithamaha Patriji, Founder of Pyramid Spiritual Societies Movement, in a meditation event organized by the masters of Chennai. Since morning that day my happiness knew no bounds and I knew it would be a big turning point in my life. As I reached the venue and saw him for the first time it was majestic—his grandeur is still indescribable for me and when I heard him say, "We are all Gods. You are a God," it went deep inside my heart, etching on my soul permanently. I never heard anyone telling that 'You are a God', I was mesmerized by his energy. I did not know how to converse with such an enlightened being.

Patriji just looked deep down into my eyes and I felt he was not looking at my physical appearance but into my soul. I was now sure; I had been waiting for him. The cherry on top was, when he said the magical words, "Carry on, you will find yourself and come to know many things." As mystical as his words were, my life truly took a 360-degree turn, beginning with the adventures towards my life-purpose. Today, I am living my life to the fullest, enjoying every moment.

After this experience, the duration of my meditation sessions increased and I started experiencing the grace of life by gaining 'Knowledge of the Soul'. In my journey so far I have learnt, 'Spiritual Science' is the only answer to every existing question, because ultimately every question ceases to exist. My heartiest gratitude to our beloved Patriji, the father figure who has dedicated his human form to make the world VEGETARIAN and spread awareness about MEDITATION with PYRAMID ENERGY.

This book is my personal journal for the reader to know my journey with MAHAVATAR BABAJI. In the year 2017, I received His message while meditating, that in the year 2018, He would enable me to channel Him to bring His life-journey out to the masses. It was October 5, 2018 when he first conversed with me directly and I could feel my soul singing with joy.

TABLE OF CONTENTS

A MAGICAL MEETING

In the year 2009, I went on a trip with Patriji along with 200 Pyramid Masters to Uttarakhand, the mostW beautiful doorway to the Himalayan Mountain Range. This trip had been planned in the divine timing by 'Masters' to Babaji's Cave.

It was my first encounter with Himalayan energies. Every place was extraordinary and all of us were re-energizing it by 'group meditation' energies with Patriji's mesmerizing flute music. While on the trip I met many wonderful masters and got introduced to 'Mahavatar Babaji' for the very first time. It was on this trip that I saw His picture and got to know the experiences of other Pyramid Masters with Him. It amazed me, and I ignited my heart to experience His presence.

Ever since I learnt about Him, there was something pulling me from the inside, perhaps my strong faith; the fire born within that told me, the Mahayogi would soon fulfill my wish to meet Him. A strong spiritual desire grew in me to see Him physically, igniting the passion in me to know the beyond.

Our group had now reached a small hamlet called 'Kukuchina' which is 53 kilometers from Ranikhet. For the night we took shelter in Dwarahat, 21 Kilometers away from Kukuchina. We planned to begin our journey to Babaji's Cave the next day after breakfast, as the journey to the cave was about 1.5 hours of trekking. Next day while I was climbing up the hills my inner voice gave me a strong feeling that Babaji would fulfill my deepest wish to meet Him that day. Thus, climbed with rapt attention, working on my awareness not to miss that beautiful meeting I was about to experience.

I had been climbing without a break so I paused and sat down on a big rock to rest for few minutes to drink water. While I was drinking from my sipper, I saw a tall woman walking towards me from a distance; she was a Caucasian woman adorned in white clothes, looking glorious. She stopped in front of me and looked deep into my eyes for a long moment while I looked back into hers and then she left without uttering a single word. I felt as if there was a pause in time at that moment as her energies and her strong presence left me with an empty mind.

I was happy but almost dizzy with this encounter. I got up and continued to trek towards the cave whilst I suddenly questioned myself, "Was this woman Babaji?" I immediately turned back to look at her, simultaneously she too turned back to look at me in that exact moment, smiling brightly with a meaningful glance — "You Recognized Me!", and disappeared into thin air after our short non-verbal exchange. I was thrilled at my experience with Babaji and my heart filled with immense happiness and gratitude. This was also my first encounter of Babaji's great shape-shifting skill.

It took 1 hour and 30 minutes of trekking time to reach the cave and after reaching our final destination we sat for group meditation and experienced a deep meditative state, as Patriji's magical flute helped us to dive deeply. In my meditation trance I saw a vision of Babaji in which He was hugging people and I could see Him standing right in front of me, showering His love on so many people, while I was a mere observer. This experience was truly a harbinger of a new dawn in my life and the beginning of my journey with Babaji's wonderful energies.

Before we walk the path of spirituality and oneness, it is difficult to believe in God and rather hard to understand the omnipresent 'God Energy'. It is only after meditation that one begins the true journey to 'Godhood' or realizing that it is all within us and not outside or externally present. Any individual introduced to Babaji may or may not believe His story. It is rather a human to doubt if a person can live in the same body for so many years. However, on the flip side of the coin, it is easier to accept that it is possible only for Mahayogi like Mahavatar Babaji, where He is telling us the truth that how it is easily possible for anyone who is ready to walk towards the higher truth. This is all a game truly, a 'game of confusion' that ends when you surrender and walk towards him.

After my first trip to Babaji's cave, His exuberant energies akin to an inevitable 'divine force' called me to this place many times, guiding me to bring along different masters to dive into adventurous experiences orchestrated by him.

In the year 2017, I revisited the caves along with young Delhi masters. After the trek we were all meditating in our cottage and I received Babaji's message saying, "Make an animation movie on my life".

"I know nothing about your life nor have I read much about your life in any book, then how can I take responsibility for such a divine task?" I asked, a little unsure. His response, however, made me smile, "I will come to you in the year 2018 and tell you my story."

While I patiently waited for Babaji's message in 2018, I was sure about one thing—everything happens in its divine right timing and so it will. Babaji is a perfect mathematician who is very accurate in his calculations. It was in the last week of September, that I received his message during meditation that he will begin his work with me on 5th October 2018. I became very curious and conscious of the journey that was about to begin. I was counting the days as I did not understand how he would start the work with me. It was just like a normal day on 3rd October 2018, when I got a vision while meditating where I saw Babaji writing on a piece of paper—"I am waiting"; I asked Him, "What is the need for you to wait, it's all yours?" "The divine wheel has its own time" He replied with a smile on his face.

It was finally 5th October 2018. I was very excited to know how Babaji would work with me this time. I waited the entire day, but to my dismay there was no experience. I finally sat in meditation to know the reason and I had a

third eye vision. A stick alighted with fire appeared before me and I entered into it. It was a different realm and I could see a huge pyramid surrounded by mist and the place was full of light. In my vision, I understood it was "KANTHI LOKAM (Light World)." As I walked towards the pyramid, I could see an orange-colored flame at its crown, slowly transforming into Babaji. He opened his eyes and said, "I will meet you in 'ATMA LOKAM' (Spirit world). I live in your mind, not in your house." After hearing His words, I bent down on my knees and clasped my hands in gratitude.

It dawned upon me the next morning that I had never kept a record of my experiences till then, due to my limited belief. I felt, because of my limited writing skills my visions would lose their essence if I start describing them. I gave up on the writing and depended heavily on my mind palace. I am an avid reader. The more I read various spiritual authors, the urge to jot down my experiences grew in my heart. But I always kept procrastinating and never really gave it a shot. This time I felt that Babaji was giving me this experience to come out of my writing block and if this was true then, I genuinely wanted to work on myself in order to fulfill the purpose.

I wanted to clear my head and decided to pay my friends a visit — I went over to Jaspreet and Prisila's house. After reaching their cozy home we sat in meditation where

I could see Babaji standing behind me saying, "Go on writing my story... You just start" He said, and I wrote His life story with an open heart, following His instructions.

Here begins my conversation with Babaji –

Pallavi: *"How is this communication happening with you Babaji? How are we connected? How was it, that the moment I opened up to receive your message, I could see you? Kindly answer."*

Babaji: *"How does it happen that two souls become one? It's just one, is it not? There is no definition or description for it. It just exists. This very moment we are communicating, we have become one although with our individualities intact. I am with you and your journey begins with me in 'NOW'."*

"In the plane of 'SatyaLokam' or 'AatmaaLokam' we are all one. A soul can vibrate with another when they both are willing to connect and share their wisdom."

Pallavi: *"Who are you and what kind of wisdom do you want to share with the world through me? Who is Shiva? Am I receiving it right, the word 'Shiva'? Please throw some light on it."*

Babaji: *"Who am I? What am I?"*

"I am the Shiva consciousness or you could say, Shiva is my over self where I have materialized to experience in the form you

identify as 'Babaji'. Wisdom is a vast term which is endless.. There is always a purpose to fulfill a particular task which can take humanity towards the truth and self-knowledge."

"I want you to write a book based on the experiences of my journey, which will reach the masses very soon. Have faith my child on what you see and hear. And always remember, 'No body and no mind'!"

Pallavi: *"Yes Babaji! I agree. I have full faith on what I see but sometimes my mind wanders and has questions.. what is the need? Why are we experiencing it? I have doubts in my physical mind and I feel there are certain fragments left that needs to clear completely."*

Babaji: *"Hmm..! Those fragments are nothing but a confusion which occurs at the meeting point of the physical and spiritual mind. But never pay attention to it because it is an obvious part of human life. Because when you start writing, how can you have judgments? You do not know what I am going to share with you. You are only following my voice in your head. Be free of doubts."*

Pallavi: *"What is this vision? Where is this path leading me to?" (Fig 1)*

Babaji: *"This path is for every soul who wants to meet me."*

Fig 1

Pallavi: *"When I connect with you and begin to write, I feel like the sound is coming from within but not from my soul, it's like a divine source. Is that right?"*

Babaji: *"You are right, it's a universal source from where everything is born but you address it as dead or death. It does not exist in the universe because it is the part of creation itself."*

"I am the source… I am Shiva Consciousness born on Earth to experience the grace of human life. I took this physical form on

Earth on March 24th 203 AD. Yes, that is my birth date."

THE VISION:

"He held a few hailstones in his hands, out of which he let go of 24 pieces. It suddenly started raining in the vision, washing away those 24 hailstones in one direction and they went through some pipe like structure. Out of 24 only 3 hailstones came out and I could finally decode it was 24th of March and His voice whispered the year 203AD."

INITIAL STEP TOWARDS SPIRITUALITY

Pallavi: "Babaji, I would like to listen to your childhood experiences."

Babaji: (smiling) "Yes, why not?"

"I was around 9 and had a big group of friends. We used to play together in a field where there was a deep well under a big Banyan tree. One day, seven of us from our group, including me, were playing. After playing we got exhausted and sat on the edge of a well. Suddenly my friend Damana tripped over and fell inside the well. Initially, we couldn't even react. All of us got scared and screamed for help. There was no one around in the scorching heat of

a summer afternoon and none of us knew how to swim. I could not just watch my friend drown, so I mustered up some courage to save him. I had no idea how would I do it, but I just jumped into the well, telling the rest of them to bring a rope which was hanging on the tree to pull us out."

"The well was deep and as I jumped inside with the aid of the rope, I could feel the cold water of the well engulfing my body. Damana was shivering because of fear and extreme cold water. I helped him to collect his strength to hold the rope till he was out of the well, not thinking about myself that moment."

"As our friends helped Damana out of the well, I had no support and my body submerged deep inside the water making me realize the adversity of the situation and fear struck my heart. It was difficult to breathe inside water. It wasn't the fear of water or the lack of swimming skills but it was the fear of death which I was facing for the first time. I flipped my hand frantically to stay afloat. I kept telling myself that if I could help Damana out of the well, I will help myself too. Something within me changed. I accepted it as a challenge, realizing there is nothing that can defeat us but our own fear. I started conversing with my body, with kindness and words of inspiration. I said aloud, 'Do not be afraid, you can learn to both swim and breathe.'

"I started drowning as my body was trying to keep afloat, fighting the water pressure in the well. I could feel death on the

threshold, trying to keep my eyes open and my heart calm, whilst programming my body continuously—it was then that I saw a bright yellow light entering the water. I got curious and tried somehow to reach the light's direction. As I approached the light and touched it I got consumed inside it as if I became the light itself. The energy it was emanating thoroughly exhilarated me and I was now swimming and breathing under water without consciously realizing it, safe in the light's cocoon. I was floating effortlessly, my eyes were closed and my breathing steady. In between this entire process, I went so deep within myself and could see someone's figure forming from that light. It disappeared as soon as it had come. I heard my friends calling my name, bringing me back to the third dimension. I had no fear any more in my heart and it was a surprise to all my friends to see me alive. I finally took the rope which my friends had thrown and came out of the well."

"I was not aware of the reality of that light source as a child but I understood that we could overcome anything merely by facing it and accepting our true unique self. This incident left an unforgettable mark on my memory. This was merely the beginning of the adventures to come."

"Few months later I had a feeling there will be a challenging situation nearing again. Besides, I was now having dreams where someone was taking me away from my land and my people. I also saw unknown faces of people who will be my students along with me in my journey to attaining true divinity. I never understood the

meaning of these dreams as I was only a child and when I shared these dreams with my mother, she ignored them saying it was a fabrication of my imagination and I must have heard some stories that had a deep impact on my mind."

"Don't worry as these visions have appeared in your dream, they will go away too," she said.

"Dreams are a very important part of your soul's journey while you are in the human form on Earth. Dreams are never vague or meaningless as every dream has its own learning value and a deep hidden message behind it. Remember, dreams show the reality of what you are in the 'Present State' and all that is yet to come, the adjacent probabilities."

"One fine day I was waiting for my friends outside a Shiva temple. It was dusk time, when I saw two men appearing from one corner of the temple. In appearance, those men differed from my village people in appearance and seemed to be outsiders. They were walking towards the other corner of the temple giving me a very weird look. Suddenly, I felt someone grabbing me from behind and covering my nose with a sweet fragrance that caused me to fade into darkness as it rendered me unconscious. I regained my senses the next day and found myself in a disorganized house. I felt dreadful that my dream had come true, the feeling I had was not a fragment of my imagination. The situation was scary for me as a child. I did not know how to come out of it—I screamed for help, however, there

was no one who could have helped me."

"They had locked the door and there was no window to plan or escape or to get help from any passer-by. It had been two days since they held me captive and nobody had come to my rescue. I was without food and water and had no hint of the whereabouts of my kidnappers. My tears had run dry and my eyes had swelled, however I found no escape. I prayed to Lord Shiva to show me a way out of the house in this situation. It was the morning of the third day; finally the kidnappers came for me and sold me to a kind gentleman. I could not understand their language as they were conversing in Bengali. However, I could make out that they had sold me to the man and he was happy to have me. The man took me to his house where his wife was waiting for us at the entrance. The moment she saw me, she overcame with motherly emotions. I never understood what transpired between them because of the language barrier. But I could understand their affection through their feelings and gestures. They were good people who loved me like their own son but in my heart I could not understand why God had put me through this situation. I was unhappy with all that was happening with me. My foster mother tried her best to keep me happy and bring a smile on my face."

"I realized soon that I was not angry with anyone for what had happened but I needed to know where this situation was leading me? Months passed and I helped my foster parents with basic household errands, besides reading books. I was paying them my sincere service

of gratitude and I could now understand their language in bits and pieces."

"As days went by and I never failed to fulfill the duties of a son. Soon my selfless act of service towards them melted my foster father's heart."

"My dear child! I know you must be missing your family and you are not happy here. I don't know where you have come from. It must be difficult for you to accept us as parents, who bought you with money. I apologize for what I did. I merely wanted to give you a great life, as you seem to hail from a good family. But with passing time,, I know I have to free you from this bondage. Today I could finally muster all my courage to have this conversation with you. Go my child, go wherever you want, he said with lot of affection in his eyes."

"Incidentally, a 'Sangha' of Yogis was passing by the house. As I looked at the congregation I felt happy within and my new parents saw me smiling genuinely for the first time. "Yogi, you must go, I have observed your nature.. and you are not a normal child. It seems your soul is longing to live this experience," my foster mother said with tears in her eyes."

"I looked at them for the last time, deep gratitude for them filling my heart and I finally walked towards the Yogis to join them in their procession."

REALIZATION OF HIGHER TRUTH

It had been two days since Babaji's last message. I was wondering what could be the cause of this delay. To understand the situation I kept checking within myself and in a part of my mind thoughts about Babaji and His story consumed me, playing a loop.

It was a usual morning that day. My husband Krishna and I got into an intense discussion about some spiritual concepts. He asked me a simple question - *"Define yourself!"*. The moment he said these words, I got furious at him thinking inside that who was he to ask me such questions and I walked away. After two hours of this episode, I was in the kitchen taking care of my daily chores. I received a message from Babaji, *"You must lock yourself in your bedroom for the next 12 hours."* I followed His instruction with no questions, confining myself in the four walls of the bedroom and began writing his story further. As I wrote, he shared something enlightening about the tiff I had with my husband in the morning. *"Calm down, this has happened with me too. It was me who was talking to you through your husband in the morning"*, Babaji revealed.

For a moment, there was complete silence and then both of us burst out laughing at the situation. I was laughing more at myself and my naivety. Feeling light in my heart, I resumed my conversation with Babaji.

Pallavi: "Babaji, shall we continue with your story further?"

Babaji: "After joining the group of Yogis, I got clarity about my purpose of life. I wanted to know more about the human life beyond this daily existence. I read the Vedas, Gita, Bible, Upanishads etc. One day, I got an opportunity to participate in a Shastrartha (a conference where people debate on philosophical or religious grounds) with a group of scholars. On knowing that I had read so extensively, one great yogi, Swami Haridas, asked me a question "If you have received command and understood everything, then tell me, how will you ***Define Yourself?"***

"I went into a deep silence, "My Silence" was an answer in itself which cannot be heard. Deliberately choosing defeat over victory, as it was a part and parcel of such debates (if an individual was quiet and crossed the time limit to respond in their defense or answer any question put across to them, they were declared defeated). However, in this situation, the answer to the question posed by Haridas was indescribable and so I was happy with my defeat."

"This incident also helped me face my 'Ahamkara (ego)' which shattered. Everything happened in a flash of few seconds and I silently walked away from the conference and began my journey towards the Himalayas. Before stepping ahead, I looked back once and saw Swami Haridas who was smiling at me. What blew my mind was witnessing a huge form of Shiva behind him. I immediately understood that the question posed at me was not from Haridas, but the super-consciousness Shiva Himself. Only one thought consumed me - I am an eternal soul and I want to be eternal in my physical form too. I was 27 years old at the time when I decided to attain the beyond of the beyond itself."

"With contentedness in heart and a smile on my face I started walking again. My true journey to the beyond had finally began. The people present there could not understand where I was heading and what path had I chosen. My face was aglow with a sense of purpose and the will to achieve something. Some disciples followed me without asking anything and others had too many questions in their head."

"My legs did not give up and I kept walking for miles, day and night covering states after states. The more I walked the more people gave up on walking with me on my journey. I carried on for days with no food in my stomach and had only liquids offered by disciples and other people on my way. The ego of pride I had developed over time by studying under the company of the most renowned Gurus of that time was false. I had felt a dire need in my soul to find my true existence. I needed to define it to myself."

"The memorable part of this journey was with one of my disciple. He walked with me in faith and true belief, no questions asked and no doubts in his heart. His name was 'Sarah'."

Pallavi: "Can you please tell me more about your disciple Sarah?"

Babaji: "Sarah was a noble soul, kind, generous and dedicated. His aim was to serve humanity. I met him in a small village at 15 years of age while visiting Sri Lanka. He was just a 7 year old boy with an innocent smile, wearing orange clothes and expressing his deep desire to be a yogi. He was always drawn to the lifestyle of a 'Sanyasi' and took great care of every yogi who visited his place, making sure he met them all. When I met him he was with his mother. Sarah got to know that a group of Yogis was visiting his village and he made sure he brought his mother along with him. They came to see us at our base camp on the open ground near the river, where we had put up our tents. I was working on some Sutras (a rule or aphorism in Sanskrit literature) with my guru, 'Divij Swami' who taught me through his sermons. Sarah met all the Yogis who were present at the base camp and finally came to meet us. As he saw me, his eyes were lit with depth and was looking at me intently."

'What do you see in me?' I asked him, my curiosity at its best.

'My Guru,' he said unperturbed.

'I feel I have waited for you for an eternity and today my search has finally come to an end. I request you to kindly take me along with you, as your disciple' he said with folded hands.

"I was surprised at his response."

"Sarah's mother smiled and said, "I have noticed the nature of a Yogi in my child. Since he was 3 year old he would feel inexplicable joy at the mere sight of a Yogi passing by. When he was 5 years of age he told me I should prepare myself for the day when his guru will come to take him along. Today the day has finally arrived and my happiness knows no bounds. I feel no pain for losing my child as I have been practicing detachment from him for the past two years. I request you to please take him along with you Guruji."

"Her clarity was impressive and I couldn't help but marvel at

the selflessness of a mother and her unconditional love for her child. I was young and my key focus was to gain more knowledge from different gurus. Divij Swami had been listening our conversation from a distance. I looked at him with many questions in my head and he simply read my eyes. His response was simple yet potent with meaning, 'Receive your first disciple and you will receive many disciples in the near future. You must not hesitate to take him with you.'

"I smiled, as Sarah touched my feet and I hugged him. That was the beginning of my journey with Sarah."

"Years went by and Sarah was always by my side. One fine day we reached a place near Badrinath. I knew this was a journey that I had to take alone and I requested him to go back to the group."

"I will come back again do not worry. This is not the end of our journey together but I have a soul purpose to attain", I lovingly conveyed to Sarah. His eyes were full of tears and there was a huge smile on his face. I saw deep love in his eyes for me which was indescribable. He folded his hands for the last time and said, "I will wait for you, until we meet again." He left, leaving an indelible mark of his kind smile and deep eyes on me."

"As Sarah left, I redirected myself to Kailas as Shiva had spoken through Swami Haridas at the conference and had instilled a renewed sense of purpose in me. I walked towards Mount Kailas

while carrying out various practices to enhance my journey on the path of truth. I had to undergo hardship and I was ready for them. I got detached from the outside world, with the sense of my physical body by performing Kriya Yoga."

"There was only one tree in the vicinity, so I chose a rock under that tree which felt magical to me. It was swaying lightly in the breeze, enjoying its surroundings. It drew me to immediately and I sat under it for my intense Sadhana. During the initial days, I could not fast for days. In the beginning my mind would pay more attention to the needs of my body and the hunger pangs. However, gradually the process reversed and I attuned with my soul, gaining control over my mind. Detachment from my body prepared it to receive energies to an extent where I did not require any food more to sustain myself. No matter, how long I walked from one place to the other I did not feel hungry at all. I realized that it was not just my soul and my mind which were in the state of knowing but also my body.. all three of them were in perfect synchronization with one another."

Pallavi: "Do you have any previous lives?"

Babaji: "Yes."

Pallavi: "Have you not taken birth after this life which we are discussing? Have you really been living in the same body?"

Babaji: "Yes, for three years I went into a deep meditative state under the tree near Kailas. Those three years enabled me to attain eternity in the same body. I got into the state of an ageless being. The massive tree protected my body for all those years. When I finally came out of my meditative state and opened my eyes, I saw the tree turning into Shiva. He poured the water of Holy Ganges on my body from His 'Jata' (matted hair). 'You must go to the souls living in the dark, craving for light. Become their soul-guide and impart them with the knowledge of Kriya Yoga,' he said and disappeared thereafter."

"My birth name was 'Nagraj' and few people also called me 'Yogi'. Lahiri Mahashaya entitled me as Babaji in the 19th Century and later many addressed me as Mahavatar."

"You can call me by any name you like. I am always close to your heart. As my body gained immortality, becoming ageless, I dropped all identities, gaining a handful of names (laughing heartily)."

"My energy frequency had reached a high level now not because of the 'Siddhis' I had attained but the great purpose I had to fulfill. I visited every individual who needed to be uplifted spiritually."

Pallavi: *"While at the Babaji caves, I got an experience where I saw you as an old man..."*

Babaji: *"Yes, true."*

Pallavi: *"But you mentioned that you are beyond age and time on this dimension — why did you not appear as a 30-year old?"*

Babaji: *"What you saw is correct because you wanted to see the age of my soul and not physical form (laughing). When you say 'You' it never refers to a body form but a soul. When you are in the physical system, you are more concerned about the body which has no meaning in the spiritual journey."*

SIRIAN BABAJI: PARALLEL LIFE EXISTENCE

Babaji: *"I was in deep meditation day and night. Reading Upanishads gave me a lot of clarity, bringing me to a zero state. When you can clean the physical debris in your mind, only then you can see the higher truth. I had truly forgotten what it was like to be in my physical body because I was journeying with my soul on a deeper level."*

THE VISION:

A ring of light rapidly traveled in space, went higher and exploded. It generated an enormous amount of light which was spreading all over; giving birth to a 'Lotus' which was light pink in color. The Lotus bloomed opening half way through and Buddha came out in front of Babaji who got up from his place of Sadhna and folded his hands in gratitude to Buddha.

"What is your role in this life?" asked Buddha.

"Kindly guide me on this aspect," Babaji replied humbly.

"You have achieved highest level of Samadhi wherein you can live in this body as long as you want, without growing older and fulfill your purpose of educating people." Buddha enlightened Babaji.

Buddha moved his right hand in a circular motion opening up a portal. He then directed Babaji to step inside the portal and work with his fellow beings to enable more energy work on Earth. Babaji nodded his head in affirmation and walked inside the portal and it closed behind him. (In the vision, Babaji was in a white dhoti and had an angvastram on his shoulders)

Babaji: "Believe in what you saw and will see. Whenever you get to see any vision that 'seeing' is nothing but your 'being'. The moment you put your physical mind in it you cannot see anything. Breathe and be free, let your soul guide you.."

CONTINUATION OF THE VISION:

Babaji was slowly walking on the path and He could see someone standing at a distance. As He reached closer to the being, He placed his hand on his shoulder and the man turned back. It was like Babaji standing in front of a mirror looking at himself. The man was an exact replica of Babaji.

He slowly changed and transformed into his original form. He was from the star "Sirius". This is how Babaji's Sirian life came into the picture to me—a parallel life experience. I could see a very tall figure, about 10 feet. He had long hair and a beautiful design on his forehead; a belt formation with pyramids on it and some blue colored crystals. He was wearing a necklace full of colorful crystals and an off-white cloth around his neck. His torso was bare and he had a cloth neatly covering the lower half of his body. His feet were big. The first two fingers of His feet were of the same size and the rest three fingers were shorter. The Sirian face was not much different from that on Earth but His skin tone was light blue and eyes were big. His name was 'Safon'.

I then saw a big eagle flying in the sky and slowly landing near Safon on the ground. It had silver color on its head and peacock blue on the rest of its body. It had an interspersed, artistic and beautiful pattern on its feathers. Babaji slowly merged into 'Safon' and they became one.

Then, Safon sat on the eagle and they took flight. The eagle was a highly aware being. They had an energy pathway in the sky, like an aerial transportation system in space, which the eagle was following as if a trained pilot. As they journeyed further, the path appeared and disappeared rapidly. Safon looked thrilled and confident whilst the sun was setting in the background announcing dusk.

Sirius has one of the biggest Suns. It is many times bigger than the Sun of Earth. The life on Sirius is more advanced than our planet and it is about 1700 light years away. The world of Sirius is more developed than that of Earth.

Safon: "I am Safon, the Sirian leader. We passionately work for the beings of Earth. I have always heard the calling of your people and I am also in contact with many of them to get my messages to Earth by the name 'SAFON'. I came down to Earth to experience it as 'Babaji', through this work we want to communicate with earthly beings directly and tell them that the truth of their existence is not different than ours. It is just that you have become so limited in your thoughts that you feel lost because you have forgotten your truth and so we are here to help you in this journey, to lift the vibrations of earth."

"It was us, the Sirians who planted Pyramids on Earth thousands of years ago. We are also the mathematical scientists

of the universe. It was because of our highly technical skills that we were able to manifest the technical assistance in the formation of pyramids. It was to raise the vibrations of Earth and help her gain higher consciousness. Every time an individual looks at the Pyramids, he wonders how these Pyramids came into existence and tries to know the secret behind it. Earth is a beautiful place for us to experiment and experience. We looked for people on Earth who could understand Pyramid concept and help others to understand the same."

"We covered the Earth with Pyramids and were waiting for the time when the human race could make giant quantum leaps in their personal journey and bring about a spiritual revolution through Pyramid Energy. We had created grid-like structures inside and outside the pyramids, invisible to the human eye, and it was built within a 2 km radius. We formed these grids for the Egyptian pyramids and every pyramid built thereafter has similar grids, you can call them 'Energy Grids'."

Pallavi: "What does this Energy Grid do?"

Safon: "Have you noticed that within the human body you have cells and the structure of these cells is also like a grid? When an Earthly being uses a pyramid—meditating under the pyramid or performing any task under a pyramid—these energy grids get connected to a human being's cellular system which are the microscopic grids of your physical body. In this entire process, when we awaken the energy grid system of the pyramids along with the human cellular system it heightens the process of raising human consciousness. We love communicating with you all but since we cannot physically visit Earth all the time we communicate with you through these pyramid energy grids. Our planet is full of pyramids everywhere. It is like a communication network from the Sirian World to that of Earth. Whenever we visit your planet, we travel through these Energy Grids which work like portals to other worlds."

"We want to see your planet living in the Light Age. Earth has already entered the Light Age but first let us understand what this light age really is."

"This Light has reached to many beings on Earth, where most of them have felt this light within. But there is still so much room for improvement. The Earth beings have lost connection with their own selves and we are here to help them."

"After the pyramids, we have a profound connection with the Earth beings through the Dolphins. Many of us from Sirius have taken life in the form of dolphins to lift the vibrations of Earth. They are one of the mediums through which we communicate with many beings on your planet. We have seen the birth of Earth and her phases through the cycle of time. She is like our second family, our second home."

Pallavi: *"Please tell me more about your home, Sirius.."*

Safon: *"Sirius is very advanced technologically, in every aspect that you can imagine. On Earth, technology is more about the devices of comfort that can make life truly easy and things accessible. However, on our star Sirius, technology is also about accessing higher soul intelligence. Our technology has guided us—we might or might not have certain devices, but we are all developed on the soul level. On top of that, our technology is not meant to destroy the nature of our home planet and is used vowing to preserve the beauty of Sirius. We all live in oneness and try to help our Sirian brothers and sisters in the same manner."*

"For us, communication is the biggest solution to everything and it is the way out. We also believe that communication is very important because everything has its own rhythm and this rhythm has its own communication. As high vibrational beings, if we want to vibrate with something or some aspect of life, we never try to convince ourselves if it can be done or not. We have gained enough patience to wait and we think it is a natural part of the same process. I, Safon, incarnated as Mahavatar Babaji to experience up-close and study it further."

"Sirians are 7th dimensional beings and we vibrate emotionally with Earth. It is close to our heart and we really love your planet. We understand deeply that every soul wants love and friendship and for this very purpose we are here with the beings of Earth.

We are here to help you understand your own emotions. We also decided to physically incarnate on earth so as to understand Earthly emotions—they are intense and complicated, but to serve the greater purpose you must learn to work around them with your own soul essence. I am living many lives simultaneously, what I am sharing with you are the words of wisdom from my parallel life existence as 'Babaji' and 'Safon'. As Babaji, I received this ancient gift of becoming one with myself and deeply understanding the knowledge of parallel life existence."

My vision shifted again, I saw Babaji slowly emerging out of Safon and walking back on the same path he had entered through the portal, back to Kailas with a sweet smile on his face.

Babaji: "My first task now is to choose a place for my work. I love to travel and cannot be at one place for long but I decided to have a place like a 'soul station' which I sought to find and thus Kukuchina became that place."

"I meditated at this place to understand the mechanism of soul work on Earth in-depth and the role I was supposed to play. Leaving my thoughts blank, I deeply meditated to meet my higher consciousness and that is how years went by. In all those years where I was meditating, my physical body became stronger, aglow with light and full of energy. I studied the science of the spiritual body for which this human body is a suit. I now hoped to meet new people

and my spiritual body helped me achieve the same."

"I will now share with you few experiences of my spiritual body work with different people."

Jaspreet and Prisila's home became the place for my soul work with Babaji and most part of the conversation with him happened here. One day, while jotting down my conversation with him, a thought came across my mind - Babaji might have chosen their home for his energy work but I also asked myself if there were more layers to this? Soon, I got a vision and I saw myself stepping down at the entrance of Mahavatar Babaji's cave at Kukuchina and I could see a route forming from Babaji's cave connecting to Jaspreet's house. It was a portal he was using as his path to travel. As the vision faded away, Babaji gave me his affable smile and asked, *"Do you still feel that you did not get your answer?"*

SOUL WORK

These are the stories that Babaji has shared through me as a medium to understand his soul work with the light workers in a gist.

STORY I

"I began my soul work from the place of my birth at Chidambaram in Tamil Nadu. I met a man named Chinmaya who was visiting my hometown for some work. He was a man with a kind heart and had a wife and two daughters."

"He was suffering a huge loss in his business and he was unhappy and looked worried. It seemed at first as though he worried

because of his dwindling business but in reality his actual concern was his soul growth in this physical life. His mind was flooded with questions, mostly those that signified existential crisis - 'What am I doing here?', 'How can I make my life worthwhile?', 'How to seek the right path?' etc."

"Dear God! Please show me the right path or else I will become weaker and sadder with each passing day. I cannot continue like this anymore and it is affecting my life and business, he yearned for the Supreme Divine to hear his call."

"I heard his inner calling and worked closely with him to help him."

VISION (SCENE 1)

Chinmaya was sitting outside a temple in silence and solitude when Babaji appeared before him disguised as a Yogi.

Yogi: *"Why are you worried?"*

Chinmaya: *(touching his feet) "I am looking for inner happiness Swamiji. This life should be worthwhile. I feel everything is worthless without a purpose and I am not able to find a direction."*

Yogi: *"Hmm... you are close to finding your true path my dear child."*

Chinmaya: *"How would I know that?"*

Yogi: *"Close your eyes."*

Chinmaya closes his eyes. Babaji touches his thumb on Chinmaya's third eye (the space between the eyebrows) and disappears. Chinmaya feels tremendous energies coursing through his body and witnesses a bright light gradually illuminating Babaji's smiling face. "You have come to me, I will take care of your soul," announces Babaji.

As Chinmaya's vision ended, he was full of energy and Babaji's smile was imprinted on his mind. Then on he started conversing with Babaji in his mind, asking questions which were most relevant for his journey.

VISION (SCENE 2)

Chinmaya was once traveling for some important work which was essential for his business to survive, however, there was so much struggle in his heart that his inner voice asked him to go deep within and seek Babaji.

The opportunity to meet Babaji arrived soon. It was a full moon night; Chinmaya was sitting in silence outside his house, staring at the moon. He was unknowingly doing Tratak (getting visions with open eyes by focusing your eyes on a particular point for a long time) and in a spectacular moment he saw Babaji appearing out of the moonlight.

"Time has come for you to know Kriya Yoga and spread it to the masses to help them realize their true soul purpose."

(Babaji kept his hand on Chinmaya's head for a few moments and disappeared as swiftly as he had appeared to meet him to put across his message.)

STORY II

I went to Sri Lanka to work with a child who needed me, a beautiful 7 year old girl waiting to meet God. It was an ordinary night when she started talking to God in her sleep. I was sitting right beside her in that moment.

Girl: *"Where are you God? I need to see you and I have been waiting for you since so long!"*

Babaji: *(keeps his hand on her head lovingly) "I am right beside you, Geeta!"*

(Geeta hears his voice deep and clear)

Geeta: *"Is that your voice? Am I hearing your voice, God?"*

Babaji: *"Yes, it is my voice." (smiling)*

"What do you want from God?"

Geeta: *"Umm... let me think..."*

"What do you look like? If you could show me your true form, I will do whatever you ask me to do…"

Babaji appears in front of her. She is surprised and happy. She walks up to him and Babaji hugs her.

Babaji: *"I am always with you, my little Goddess!"*

STORY III

Babaji was once in Nepal. The scene in my vision is that of a forest. He is walking in the forest and decides to rest under a big tree and sit for a while. A bright light is radiating from His body, His presence is serene attracting little animals—rabbits, dogs, sheep, birds, etc. He happily plays with them and pets them with love and kindness. I see a herd of sheep that has come to visit Babaji. After a few moments, a man comes looking for his sheep, slightly angry at them to have wandered off so far. As soon as he reaches the tree, he becomes calm and feels a miraculous energy around. His emotional oneness with Babaji automates his body and he sits down near the tree, unaware of Babaji's presence, for he couldn't see him with his human/physical eyes.

He eventually falls in a deep slumber, his head lying on the Mahayogi's lap. Babaji places his hand on the shepherd's head, smiling lovingly. The astral body of the shepherd projects out of his physical body, now clearly seeing Babaji. As he sees the divine yogi caressing the head of his physical body it overtakes him with emotions.

"Please bless my soul," the Shepherd requests earnestly to Babaji. Babaji lifts his hand in Baba Mudra and replies with a huge smile on his face, *"Take care of the animals. Love them, protect them. Those who are killing these innocent beings, stop that business and the animal kingdom will bestow their unconditional love and gratitude upon you. These animals will serve your livelihood."*

Babaji disappears into thin air activating another light worker to continue on his path.

CAVE ADVENTURES

There are many adventures that your life will engage you in, but there are few that will stay with you like an indelible mark on your soul—Babaji asked me to share such experiences with all of you.

Once I went to a trip along with the Delhi team to Babaji's cave. The young masters from Delhi sat in chain meditation at Dwarahat. I got an experience where I saw a huge wheel with three portions, out of which two portions were held by Babaji and Patriji respectively. The hands of all the 'Divine Masters' who came down to visit Babaji's cave held the third portion of the wheel *(Fig 2)*. In this vision, the hands of our beloved masters signified the contribution of energy flow on Earth.

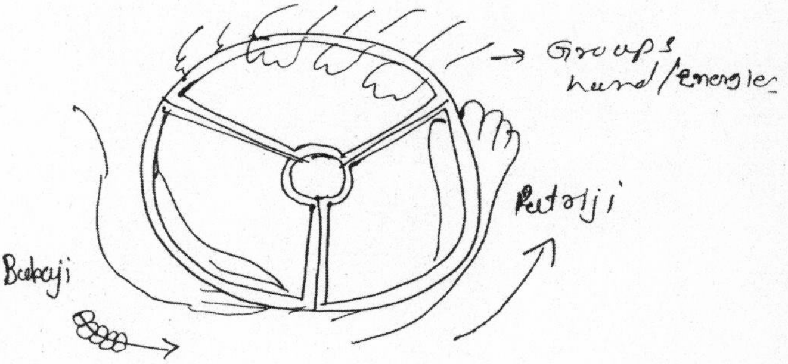

Fig 2

The vision shifted and now Babaji and I were sitting facing each other. The people around me went deep in their meditation and released their astral bodies which merged into Babaji's hair. He folded his hair into a bun and said, "Come and meditate tomorrow in the caves, I will then guide these souls back. Until then, they are with me."

The next morning we started for Kukuchina and it took us around two hours to reach the entrance of the cave. Again all of us sat in chain meditation and we could feel a tremendous amount of energy flowing within. The wheel from my previous vision appeared again and it was now at the center of the circle which were formed for meditation. When I first saw the wheel as it reappeared, felt some turmoil beneath it, like an undercurrent. As the vision took me deeper I realized that the undercurrent was nothing but the formation of a new galaxy, happening beneath the Cave *(Fig 3)*. The energy work we were doing would have led to the release of this new galaxy into the Universe.

Fig 3

This time I could actually know the true essence of the cave and how big it was from the inside. Incidents in the past, where few people had lost their way inside the caves, had led to closing down a majority area of the cave keeping only the entrance of the cave open to the public. I saw a long tunnel like route that led deep inside the caves. It was a long route. In my vision I saw few skeletons lying around and I could decipher immediately that they were the physical remains of the Yogis who had performed great Sadhana, vacating their physical forms in this place.

I then witnessed a magical world in the cave—there was a bright light almost at the end of the cave tunnel and this light was dazzling at the center-point, intersecting into two new pathways within the cave. This was the exact area where there was a scientific laboratory. This sacred place was the energy work station for the new galaxy formation. Now I realized the true purpose of the wheel vision, this energy flow—the combined energy of Babaji, Patriji and all the Divine Masters was necessary to help release this galaxy in the Universe. Our group along with other soul groups was also a part of this galaxy formation. I now understood my true purpose of coming here along with Delhi Masters on a specific trip. I saw the energy of our group being channeled to the wheel as we continued our chain meditation, moving the wheel like a tiny cosmic shift.

In life nothing happens without a reason, all we need is a thirst to find it. Every time I visit Babaji's divine cave in the Himalayas, it brings me immense pleasure and a satisfaction of experiencing his wisdom and satisfying energies of the very place itself. It is like a green carpet of beautiful energy all over.

Let me rewind the time-line, to share an amazing experience which I had in the year 2011. Everyone was meditating inside the cave but I decided to meditate outside the cave. In just few seconds I was into deep meditation as the energies were divine and flowing like a current. I saw some turmoil in the weather and the sky went grey. I saw a portal forming in the sky and a group of divine souls coming out of it. There were around 15 in number who just landed in front of me.

I was numb, shocked and surprised trying to collect my thoughts. Their energies were so godly, filled with great joy and love overflowing from my soul for them. I could not help but marvel at the group.

A man from the group came face to face with me. He was carrying something which looked like a treasure box. He was perhaps the leader of that group. He stood in front of me with a gentle smile on his face and handed me a box.

He whispered, "I am giving this treasure box to you which has 10 gifts. You need to give it to 10 people who deserve it. Until then you have to take care of this box." he whispered.

I responded with an inevitable question from a human mind, *"How would I know who these people are?"*

"You will come to know when you meet them," he told me confidently.

After handing over the box they returned to the same portal and disappeared. Later, I got to know through my vision of Babaji's Sirian existence, that the man was none other than 'Safon' himself! I was so amazed to witness the divine game—how things happen in bits and pieces and eventually when we put everything together, we get a clear picture.

Pallavi: "Babaji! I request you to kindly throw light on the energy work happening within your cave..."

Babaji: "This place is a 'space station' where the beings of other realms can land safely into the Earth zone. Many yogis have performed their Sadhana in my presence to gain soul knowledge. I have witnessed over 5000 Yogis meditating here for years at a stretch. It was only in the beginning of the 20th century that some local folks obstructed the entry to the womb of my cave out of fear."

VISION: (TRAININGS ON THE OTHER SIDE)

Babaji was in a deep meditative state along with many souls sitting in front of him. He slowly came out of his transcendence and looked at the beings sitting in front of him. He got up from his place and walked around as everyone else slowly opened their eyes.

"We are coming down on Earth in physical body to know and understand the things which lies beyond.. but one must have the faith to behold it all in a deep understanding. Do not be afraid of your thoughts and what you experience. Faith will not travel from one end to the other. You must remember, it is within you like a little child playing hide and seek. If you do Sadhana, you will train this child to grow and nurture it further with your devotion as your wisdom matures along with it. Develop faith in whatever you do and you will find me assisting on your path."

After delivering the words, he sat back on his place and other souls who were seeking his teachings touched His feet, for blessings. As the souls came to seek His blessings one after the other he could see their future and path for their soul's work. In my vision, I saw these souls approaching Babaji; one of them was Lahiri Mahashaya and the other was Yukteshwar Giri, the next Yogananda and so on... He smiled fondly, blessing them all and said, *"I will see you all physically when you incarnate on Earth at the right time."*

MISCELLANEOUS QUESTIONS

The Following Vision Describes Babaji Becoming One with Nature.

Babaji was playing Ghatam (matka) and seemed to be great by producing music with the tap of his fingers. He was enjoying himself thoroughly, as if He was nature himself. Stunning beautiful birds were flying in the sky as if dancing in celebration. As he played the melodious tune, many forest animals gathered around him—small and large animals, there was also a tiger there and it was magical to witness all.

Babaji: *"I am a Jyoti which spreads light to a limited area in its surroundings, when the oil-soaked cotton wick is lit. The moment a soul decides that it is not a Jyoti but an infinite light itself.. then it leaves the flame behind to merge into infinite light. The mind is mischievous; it will always trick us on the path specifically towards which is not right for our soul."*

"I am the infinite light'—as much as I realize this ultimate truth, I also realize that truth in this moment is I am still a Jyoti."

I have to kindle this Jyoti in everyone's heart. They also would then realize and understand their experience as a soul. Every soul is progressing towards infinite light, there is no doubt about it.. but on this path I am moving as a Jyoti. To illuminate many Deep and make them aware of their own light by taking them closer to their experience of the same; that is my soul purpose.

'Deep' needs oil to keep it burning...similarly, to illuminate your soul the science of meditation is extremely important. Without this the illumination of Jyoti is not possible. The wick which is being burnt is our mind, the oil symbolizes meditation practice, Sadhana.. the illuminated 'Deep' is our soul. Through the practice of meditation our mind is lit, implying that the mind becomes strong while being trained with pure and worthy thoughts. The light from this Jyoti enables the growth for soul's knowledge by sharing itself as much as possible (Fig 4).

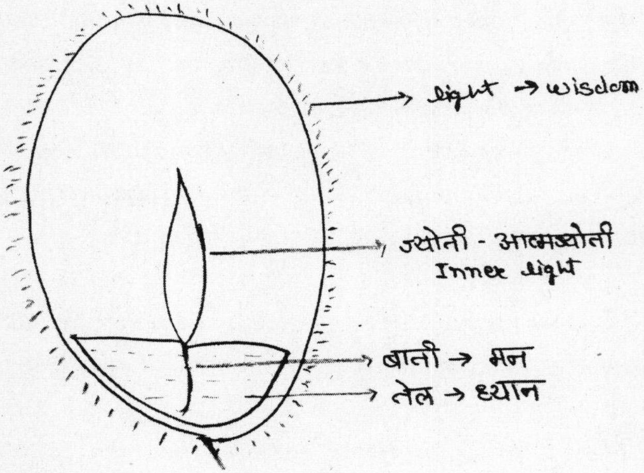

Fig 4

<u>*Pallavi*</u>*: "Please enlighten me, why is it that I receive you with clarity on an empty stomach, especially after the morning stomach cleansing routine?"*

<u>*Babaji*</u>*: "A yogi should always maintain awareness on the subject of his Sadhana. Till now people have come into the lap of the Himalayas to do intense penance .Those who are following the Middle Path and staying in societies for carrying out mass welfare like you must do Dhyanasadhana (meditation practice) but apart from the practice of Dhyan, the next aspect which is of utmost importance is to clean the body and mind".*

"Never consume food more than half your appetite. The body of a yogi must always feel light. You do not realize why you feel

heavy after eating a full stomach. It is because you are in a habit of eating more than required. When you sleep at night and wake up early in the morning for bath, in that process whatever action or karmas you have done in the previous day gets cleansed to bring your consciousness into purity for the present day which is extremely essential."

"When your body digests food it releases energy, thus the body prepares itself to receive new energy. In order for you to receive me, you must be free of previous, day karmas to experience my energies anew. This aspect of the body influences the mind immensely. If you want to keep your body in a conscious receiving state, then consume the right sattvik food and eat only as much as is needed, this will ensure that you can realize and understand your soul experience at deeper levels."

Pallavi: "Earlier, you mentioned that you can speak 21 different languages. What all languages can you speak Babaji? Would you kindly talk more about it?"

Babaji: "I can speak any language as I have become one with nature and with any soul whom I come across. However, what I have told you is true... I have learnt 21 languages from different people and have a good command over them."

"These are Tamil, Hindi, Garhwali, Dutch, Spanish, English, Hebrew, Urdu, Taiwanese, Mandarin, Mayan, Canadian,

Pawnee, Malay, Bihari, Turkish, Sanskrit, Pali, Portuguese, Nigerian, Bengali etc. Soul needs no language but only mind does. Communication between two souls is nothing but a vibrational meet-up."

"I have worked with many but all could not receive me. It is like your work where you process an email. Some may receive it on time and respond whereas some may see it late. There will be someone who may never see it and delete it thinking it to be spam or junk."

"To have this soul-communication one must vibrate on the energy frequency of receiving. For this we must train our minds. I only begin my work with the souls when they are on receiving frequency. As I enable them, they can enable others too in the process."

SECRET BEHIND PHYSICAL IMMORTALITY

Babaji: "Virtual immortality is the deepest ignorance of mankind"

Pallavi: "Kindly throw some light on it, Babaji!"

Babaji: "On one hand, your so called 'science' has developed immensely over these years getting people closer and on the other hand, man-made technology has also developed enormous ignorance."

Pallavi: "From where is this ignorance born?"

Babaji: "There is no particular place except 'mind' which gives birth to this ignorance. Human mind is the only tool which goes on developing both positive and negative sides of the coin. External mind should turn inward.. only then it will experience the self and wisdom of one's own experiences. Your world has become digital but it's all so foolish; because you desired to have this foolishness. This foolishness results from ignorance and people are now enjoying life powered by robotic technology, thinking it is the reality."

"The phrase 'Physical immortality' sounds like a newly coined term which is an area of research to explore, for so called developed technological minds.. but the truth is, it has never been surprising for those who have developed and gained the ability to explore their inner self."

"When you look deep inside, you understand that the soul itself is immortal. One gets inner sounds of "I am immortal" reverberating like waves in their very core. But when you open your eyes and get into the physical world you feel difficult to experience the same feeling. So what exactly is happening here?"

"Body, mind and soul are never a separate entity but One. When you bake a cake you put different layers to it; you decorate it, put some icing on it and use different flavours in the batter and finally when it's ready you call it a chocolate cake or a butterscotch cake, so on and so forth... Similarly, 'YOU' or 'I' or the 'SOUL' is never a separate entity at all."

"When one realizes this and lives in it completely they can experience this higher truth of living in the same body as long as you want it. Do not differentiate between physical life and spiritual life, it is the same."

"However, this entire truth of the mind, body and soul being one entity varies for the people who are ignorant or not enlightened enough where they need to get closer to their true inner-self to understand this ultimate truth."

ENERGY OF BELIEF

Pallavi: "Could you please talk more about belief?"

Babaji: "One should allow the energy of belief in one's life. I have seen many centuries on this Earth out of which "HUMAN" is such a being or you can say the only beings, who need to get educated about themselves and especially about belief energies because this whole existence lives in this energy only."

"Our Mother Earth who has offered this beautiful creation to manifest, basically exists on this 'belief energy'. The human mind has always wondered how the Earth is a ball hanging in space. Now you have found the scientific answer to it but the truth is that

she is living only on this invisible energy called belief."

"She believes she can live...

She believes she can create...

She believes she can feed..."

"Just imagine, what will happen if Earth just loses this belief? You cannot even imagine ......hahaha!"

"The power of belief is always an ever-expanding process. Just allow this energy inside you and you will get to see the miracles happening all around. How does a seed turn into a plant? How do birds leave their babies as soon as they know how to fly? How do clouds know that plants need water? This is all happening just because they never stopped believing in themselves and others too. But humans have lost this miraculous and powerful energy. Now the whole game is to re-build this again and again... till you live in this truth completely."

"It is alive deep down in everyone but the human mind needs to understand this with absolute awareness. You carry this energy of belief on and off but cannot achieve success until you seek and begin spiritual practices. Now let's see what happens when you allow this energy of belief inside of you."

"This energy you are born with, lives within as a child but you lose it as you get the capacity to think, entering into the world of thoughts. You get occupied in building your thoughts and desires, losing the belief energy."

Pallavi: *"What do you mean here by losing belief energy?"*

Babaji: *"Good question. Losing belief energy means losing the sense of seeing the world inside out. You believe by taking external perceptions and their effects inside, which is mostly dealing with both truth and untruth.. no matter even if all the time you may think it to be the truth. In short, you are developing some belief system all the time, in all your different incarnations."*

"All the time you play this game of belief. Many of you don't even believe that you have developed a false belief system. As one meets their self they break their old patterns of beliefs and build new ones… again breaking the old one and building the new one. This process just goes on and on."

"This is how you walk the path of truth by developing your belief system based on the realization of your soul."

Babaji: *"Is it that your belief following your thoughts or is it that your thoughts are following your belief?"*

Pallavi: *"Our thoughts follow our belief system."*

<u>Babaji</u>: *"Right!"*

"The development of belief energy happens more with the knowledge of soul and you will find this energy becoming very strong by experiencing the truth of one's life. You can call this as a form of 'SURRENDER'. Now this energy of surrender has many degrees. To experience this journey, one should become a Yogi."

<u>Pallavi</u>: *"Please give your message for the youth to attain their true 'Divine Self'."*

<u>Babaji</u>: *"Right from our childhood, we pray to God and we remember the Almighty in every situation. As we grow up, it becomes more as a calling game...we give a lot of calls to God most of the time unknowingly. When you are in youth it becomes a process, a subconscious act. Here, we need to sow the seed in the right manner to awaken their own God rather than calling an external God whom you never know. Present era is the digital era. It is the age where everyone has become aware of new things very quickly and any news spreads like a wildfire."*

"The time has come now for Earth where divinity of everything will take everyone close to their soul-knowledge. Especially the youth are waiting for their own divine call from their own God within. Humanity has preserved the ethical culture of their ancestors but forgotten to understand the depth. However, now you can see youth have gained wonderful insights from within and from the creations

which were predicted even centuries back in ethical texts."

"If you would have observed saints or spiritual leaders, they got this divinity of self during the period of their youth and not at old age. It shows how important the time of young age is. The first message for the Youth to attain the divine nature is Sajjan-sangatya (company of self-realized, like-minded people). The youth are lost in the environment they are living in, confused in choosing between right and wrong. Only the company of self-realized minds will help them get closer to their own divine nature."

Pallavi: *"Why are you named as Mahavatar? Is it because of the Siddhis you have attained or is there more to this story?"*

Babaji: *"Who is an Avatar?"*

Pallavi: *"One who takes a human form for the sake of humanity, to teach and to show them the path; incarnation of a supreme divine soul in a physical form on Earth."*

Babaji: *"Well said. As I have mentioned earlier that I am Shiva consciousness. Shiva is known as 'Mahadev' which means God of the Gods, one who has achieved the greatness of the great. I am an incarnation of his beloved snake, Vasuki."*

"I am the Avatar of Vasuki who is the very part of Shiva himself. This is the major reason why people on Earth who have seen me or

had experiences with me, feel impossible to achieve what I have and find it unusual. I am like a Hero to them, their Superman. The power I gained, the siddhis, sounds like magic to people. However, it is not magic, it is metaphysical science. To understand it, one must gain knowledge on metaphysics."

Pallavi: *"True. But it is truly a wonder to see you are living for the last 1800 years in the same body. Have you not felt bored in it ever?"*

Babaji: *(laughing) "Bored with what? The same body you mean or life?"*

Pallavi: *"Both.."*

Babaji: *"I have no time to get bored. I live in No Time concept. I am a Soul, a higher consciousness who stepped in the physical system and this system runs in my mind and soul, I never think of the body except to take good care of it. There is tremendous work ahead to raise the consciousness of Earth. Not only for me but it is a responsibility of all beings to walk towards the light."*

"However, only self-realized beings will understand this responsibility in its depth. Therefore, my purpose is to help mankind in the process of self-realization. After this, whatever one attains in due course, they will walk on their own path towards truth and purpose."

Q & A WITH BABAJI

Himangi Belsare, Pune

Himangi: "What and when will be the turning point for humanity in the direction of the long awaited Golden Age?"

Babaji: "You are in Golden Age itself. What happens when you leave your house and go for a long vacation? When you come back, you have to clean your house so that the new energies can enter. Golden Age has already begun, but it will take time to come to the forefront because of the process of ongoing cleaning."

Himangi: "What about the rest of the world? When will their transition begin? Any message for me?"

Babaji: "They are in the process of transition which is negligible as of now, work is happening behind the scenes. There are several groups working to make it happen on the other side. Yes, it is a little difficult for all to reach the higher state and understand the same.. but the goal is ultimately self-realization for every human on Earth, which will happen for sure and those who cannot come to terms with it, cannot stay in this vibration."

Babaji: "And yes, no guidance as you are already doing everything perfectly."

Himangi: "Thank you so much."

SWATHI PONNALA, CHANDIGARH

Swathi: "Babaji, I now knew that the purpose of my life is to share what I know. How can I get more clarity about the same?"

Babaji: "The whole game of life is to seek clarity in whatever we do. That's a part of the process which is never-ending. One must understand that, once you get clarity about what you do then you should continue to work in that discipline.. and that discipline will take you closer to your higher life purpose. What you are doing is already perfect; just keep doing your work to gain more depth."

Swathi: "How to balance physical and spiritual life?"

Babaji: "There is no need to 'balance' as such. Are you trying to 'balance' Earth and Sky? No, you can't. Because those energies will take care of themselves. In the similar manner, physical life will take care of itself and spiritual life on its own. Don't differentiate them because it is not so. For a Yogi everything is spiritual. Every act you do or perform becomes spiritual due to the expansion of your consciousness. Just fulfill your hunger for knowledge by sharing with others what you have experienced in different lives and in different roles. That is all."

Swathi: "Thank you for this deep clarity."

Alisha Netalkar, Goa

Alisha: "How can I heal completely from my mental illness (OCD, Depression and Anxiety) that I suffer from?"

"I have been unable to detach from my past lover who

was very dear to me and helped me initially in my recovery. Is our relationship over for good? If so, how can I move on? I feel discomfort in my solar plexus while I am saying this."

Babaji: "Hmm... There is no physical illness as such."

Alisha: "No physical illness?"

Babaji: "Everything is born from mental illness. It's not about detachment but learning... how will you detach till you know why you have attracted such an experience in life? Life always has a new plan and if you believe this you have to leave old energies behind to accept new energies. This is understanding about love in true sense. He gave you this enriching experience which might be full of happiness and sadness in your life. In reality, however, he helped you to move on. Thank his soul and move on; find the right person for your life. When you heal past wounds and welcome your new life all your discomforts will disappear too."

Alisha: "Hmm... I will remind myself of this. Thank you."

Babaji: "Will you cry when the show of a movie is over?"

Alisha: "Hahaha... I don't think so."

Babaji: "Then why now? It is over, get ready to see new one."

Alisha: "Great! I needed to know this."

Babaji: "Forgive and forget."

Alisha: "Thank you so much, I will apply this in my life."

BHARGAV REDDY, ANDHRA PRADESH

Bhargav: "From past one month I am feeling that my body does not need food. Even after two days of fasting I am not feeling hungry. Why am I feeling like this?"

Babaji: "Hmm… Your soul is working hard on other planes and less conscious on the physical plane because your physical body is trying to support your astral learning. It will demand food on its own as your consciousness comes back completely in this physical body. So be it."

Bhargav: "Thank you, Babaji."

RAJESH KHELE, PUNE

Pallavi: "Hello Sir I Just received a message from Babaji that he will be with you this Thursday!"

Rajesh: "I am desperately waiting to be with Babaji. What do I have to do? Please guide."

(Babaji comes instantly and start conversing,)

Babaji: "Have faith… be with me. Have faith in such a way it will not have a single spark of unfaithful thought. It will reach your soul's core where everything and anything is possible."

Rajesh: "Any message for me Babaji?"

Babaji: "Put all your heart in me and you will have no worries even to think about... This project will give you ideal ways to work with your highest intelligence with a strong emotional background within. What will you offer me? (smiles)"

Rajesh: "Whatever I have in this life and all my past lives are yours."

Babaji: "Just offer me your faith."

Rajesh: "Fully, always. I am in deep gratitude."

SHUBHAM TRIPATHI, PATNA

Shubham: "I meditate every day for 30 minutes and I love to meditate. But after meditation my body gets pain in some parts and I feel very uncomfortable. When I stop meditation for a few days I don't feel that pain or discomfort. I began to feel that spirituality does not want me to dive in. Please guide me Babaji."

Babaji: "What happens when a woman carries her baby for nine months, doesn't she go through all the pain and discomfort during that period? The new energy which she carries in her womb grows day by day and she handles all of this with great patience. She knows how much she needs to face the pain. She knows about the struggle to grow new energy in her body that will grant her a great fruit soon after this period."

"This is also the same with Dhyanam. When you meditate you are receiving new energy in your body system and this energy is doing the work of cleansing your different body parts. Have patience to see this pain and be free."

Shubham: "Ji Babaji!"

RADHIKA MEHROTRA TAUNK, NEW DELHI

Radhika (to Pallavi): "Di, as you share this one particular incident that you had mentioned about Babaji leaving for Kailas where he sat under a particular tree which protected him for the years where he practiced to do his 'Sadhana'... I dreamt about it yesterday, exactly as you were describing it a few moments ago..."

"Snowcapped mountains surrounded the tree. I could see a huge form of Shiva, which was nothing but that tree whilst I saw Babaji sitting under that tree in the form of someone really close to me. Could you please throw some light on it? I cannot believe my ears; you had just shared an experience I saw in my dream…"

Babaji: "Yes, you are my little Champ!"

Radhika: (astonished as Babaji speaks to her directly through me) "I did not get you, Babaji?"

Babaji: "In your past life, you were 'Sarah', my disciple."

Radhika: "I bow down to you Babaji!" (tears of gratitude and recognition)

KEYS TO DEVELOP SELF-AWARENESS

In this digital world, everyone is getting more awareness about the things happening around the globe. However, in this process we have forgotten to take care of ourselves spiritually. On one side many people are getting inspired to know more about themselves; to find their purpose in life and on the other hand, people are also going astray.

When I started my journey towards truth and my life purpose I implemented few things on myself to raise my awareness. I am sharing with you all what I gained from my Guru Brahmarshi Patriji's teachings and through self-experience.

1. 10 MINUTES ENERGY BREAKFAST

Food is a very important aspect of human life where most people are concerned about feeding the physical body. If we think about it deeply, the body gains only 5 % of energy through food, but where does the rest 95% come from?

People receive energy while in a state of deep sleep. The cosmic energy we receive during our sleep, combined with the energy we get through food helps us to survive the years we live. However, these energies are not enough for a day to stay healthy and happy.

When I understood the real concept of meditation and began Anapanasati, I truly understood what 'energy' actually meant. In my initial days, whenever I used to get time I followed the procedure of crossing my legs, clasping my hands, closing my eyes and observing the natural flow of my breath for 10 minutes. I did not mind the place or my surroundings, I just sat and meditated and it gave me a fresh feeling every time and a newer perspective.

At least 10 minutes or more every day to self will change a lot of things within us and everything will take care of its own. You will love to eat this energy breakfast more and more with practice. I call this a 10-minute energy breakfast and I thoroughly enjoy indulging in it.

As we receive universal energies in our mind and body, it recharges our soul, where it starts opening new doors to every situation you face. The present generation is quite advanced and most of them are gaining enough awareness to see their wrong doings but failing to implement. This 'energy breakfast' will offer them to replenish their power of discernment and with daily practice they will achieve a great journey of transformation within and around. They will gain more positive energy that influences your surroundings.

2. CHECK IN AND CHECK OUT

We check in on Earth as we have taken physical birth on this three dimensional reality and we physically check out when we vacate the body or 'physical death'. This process of check-in and check-out is like a lifelong thing as long as you are in this physical body. If you enter a particular situation you will exit from it too. But have you ever pondered upon your thoughts? There is only entry and seldom exits from thought patterns! We keep accumulating and revising them again and again whilst there is no doorway to exit. This is a very important and serious matter to think about and requires an immediate exit action plan.

I practice this consciously along with my 10-minute Energy Breakfast routine. Every night before I go to sleep, I just close my eyes and sit quietly; relax myself, then put few simple questions to myself, "Have I done something unnecessary today, any action which was not required? Have I spoken any unwanted words? Is there any situation that made me feel guilty? How would I like to see myself as a being?" If I need some improvements on my action and words, automatically the area of rectification appears in front of me. This helps me develop acceptance towards my deeds and my transformation process becomes more effective and easy. At first, it may sound hard to you or it might bring out the non-acceptance towards your own present Karma, but if you follow this for a week you will understand and receive its benefits.

On one hand, this small exercise of check-in will help you clear all the garbage, which you have accumulated subconsciously. This cleansing process will help you become a new person as well as help you to gain a newer perspective on self. You will feel more confident within.

Who is a successful person?

In my perception, people who are highly successful are those who can sleep every day with no guilt or complaints about themselves. As we are open to receive all through regular check-in and check-out process, everything in our life starts changing and it becomes more fulfilling.

3. DO NOT REACT

We always react to situations both externally and internally, especially internally. To gain any semblance of a situation it is important to go within to respond and not to react. Most of the chaos happens because we react, as all that is happening inside disturbs our mind and our thoughts, poisoning our attitude towards self and others. Develop your thought pattern in a way which will not allow any external thought to poison you before you have the entire picture of the situation clear to you. You ought to play the role of a pure observer.

For instance, if your boss is unhappy about your work and tells you that you are not doing well, rather than allowing the degrading thoughts about self, think "where you are lacking?". An area of improvement needs to be taken care of and only then you will be able to get a solution to perform better. However, if you react and go on a spree of degrading thoughts and putting yourself down, you are allowing the lower energies to take over you and your surroundings.

Remember, you are the owner of your house, body and mind. If you are allowing someone or something to go inside, only then it will affect you. In most cases, people are so affected by these energies, they become depressed or go in a state of numbness—also called a psychic attack, which means that the individual who is affected, allowed someone or something to affect them in such a severe manner.

The best way to protect yourself is to not react but respond. Even if you have allowed the negative energies inside and have become low, you can always gain confidence through the energy of the Universe by practicing MEDITATION. Even if you have been paralyzed spiritually by a psychic attack or unwanted negative energies, you can always jump back on track.

It is difficult to always respond and not react because human nature is driven by emotions, especially the negative ones.. the ultimate cure to this is practice, the more you practice forgiveness and responding to situations, the more clarity you will get.

4. DREAM OBSERVER

Dream is not just a dream.. it's a reality in the astral world. Your thoughts manifest quickly as a reality on the astral plane. When you observe your dreams your learning becomes quicker and this way the time required to receive any knowledge is reduced by working on your dreams within yourself.

When you seek to become an observer you will see and understand the real truth. You will learn that you are the source of all the things that are happening through you.

It does not matter, if you remember all your dreams or not, just work with at least one of your dreams to begin your work.

You will get lot of insights about yourself. A great transformation will take place within, by working with your dreams. Gradually, you will break the pattern of day-dreaming or lose imagination as you would have gained a higher level of consciousness of your subconscious mind.

5. Reading

I was an average reader before realizing my true self. I became a voracious reader, after I understood that the ultimate truth differed from this physical reality in which we are living.

I couldn't live without books. Reading at least one page a day is food for my intellect. I got introduced to a huge number of spiritual books recommended by Grand Master Brahmarshi Pitamaha Patriji. He always encourages people to read as much as they can. He says "Books are the swiftest shortcut to Enlightenment", so I developed a habit to read books which helped me to shine my inner world.

Books are your closest friends. Whatever you are going through in day-to-day life challenges, you will always find a book in a home that will help you to find your peace within. They help you to conquer your inner thirst for knowledge. By reading books of various authors, the knowledge you will gain will lift your intellect to a higher state of consciousness. In my personal experience of reading books, it had turned out to be a great adventure. I would connect to the author of the particular book and would get more information from them rather than that given in the book.

Read a page a day and keep your worries away, exactly how an apple a day would keep the doctor away!

6. IT IS NOT YOURS

In life we always think that there is so much which we don't understand and we wonder "What is there for us?"

When we see the external world through our physical eyes.. the world glitters and we often lose ourselves thinking we own it all. However, it is important for us to dive within to actually understand that out of all that we have there is much more and beyond than the material world.

Universe always helps us through the right opportunities but we fail to realize lessons from it. People around you speak about what they have achieved. They tell you what is convenient for them by making you believe that it is also right for you.. but the same formula never applies to everyone as each individual experience is unique.

It may sound difficult because we pick up different experiences when learning more about our own self to gain the right understanding through those unique experiences. As you get the clarity of what is and what is not for you, you also learn to say 'No' to what does not serve you in your life purpose. This is how you will find clarity to serve your true purpose.

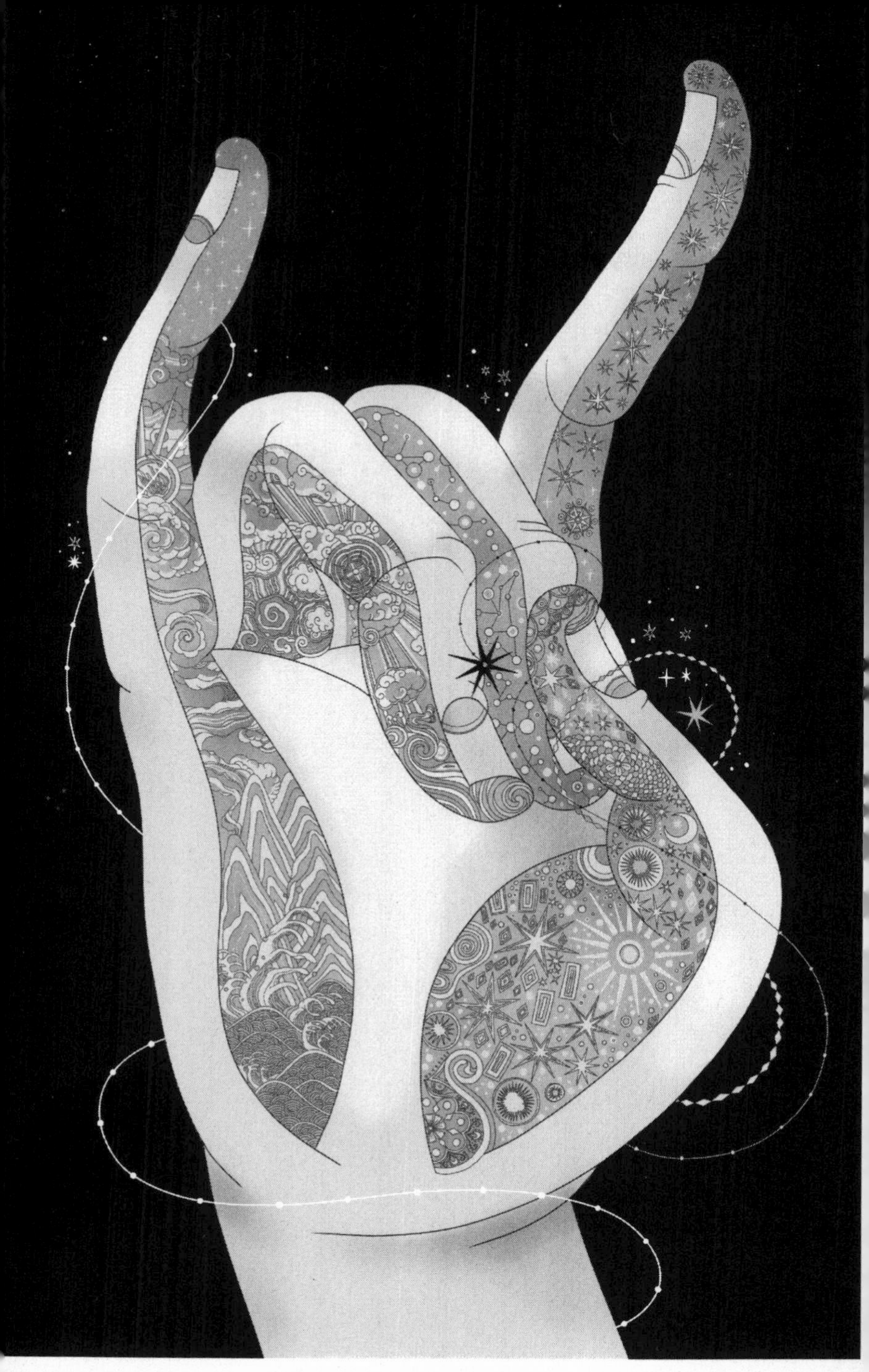

CONCEPT OF BABAJI MUDRA

As explained by **Brahmarshi Pithamaha Patriji**, Founder, Pyramid Spiritual Societies Movement, India.

The HUMAN HAND has five fingers.

- Little finger
- Ring finger
- Middle finger
- Index finger
- Thumb finger

These different fingers symbolize different concepts in the field of SPIRITUAL SCIENCE.

- Little finger - Physical Body
- Ring finger - Mind
- Middle finger - Intelligence
- Index finger - Cosmic Self
- Thumb finger - Supra-Consciousness

"THE PHYSICAL BODY"

We obtain the PHYSICAL BODY from the physical parents and the Earth elements. PHYSICAL BODY is the minimal part of the totality of our Self. That is why it is represented by the LITTLE FINGER.

When we were a kid, we used to show the little finger to depict he nature's call...

The 'LITTLE FINGER' represents the PHYSICAL BODY.

"THE MIND"

When two hearts and two minds meet and vibrate at the same frequency, there is a marriage in effect, and they exchange the rings only on the RING FINGER and not on any other finger...

THE MIND is obtained from the indoctrination of the Society. If we grew up in a Hindu family, we will have a Hindu mind. If we are born and brought up in a Christian family, we will possess a Christian mind, so onWW and so forth.

* * *

Further, the RING FINGER is much bigger than the little finger, indicating that the "MIND" is more important than the "PHYSICAL BODY".

THE MIND, in fact, is the total controller of the physical body.

The 'RING FINGER' represents the Mind.

"THE INTELLIGENCE - BUDDHI"

THE INTELLIGENCE - BUDDHI differentiates between good and the bad; truth and the untruth; right and wrong; correct and incorrect; propriety and impropriety; beautiful and ugly – irrespective of the factors in a SOCIETY.

Whereas THE MIND is automated through the social conditioning and prejudiced, the INTELLIGENCE - BUDDHI is less prejudiced and less biased.

The Intelligence is the sum-total distillate of all the Experiences of a Soul, encompassing all its karmas, in all its different lifetimes and Existences.

Experiences from all our previous lifetimes become the SOURCE—NUCLEUS of the present Intelligence. THE INTELLIGENCE – BUDDHI is the END RESULT of the totality of Soul's 'heaven time' and 'Earth time' history.

We observe that the MIDDLE FINGER is bigger than the ring finger. THE INTELLIGENCE is far greater than THE MIND.

The totality of all life experiences is far greater than this life experience and the society's general thinking.

The 'MIDDLE FINGER' represents the INTELLIGENCE.

"THE INDIVIDUAL SELF"

When we point out somebody, we use the INDEX FINGER, not any other finger!

In fact, we are not just our physical body; we are not just our mind; we are not just the intelligence. We are the soul, the Atma—the cosmic self

"ATMA" is nothing but an eternal speck of Consciousness, Energy and Wisdom!

The Individual Self is otherwise called as "Jeevatma".

The 'INDEX FINGER' represents the INDIVIDUAL SELF.

"THE COSMIC SELF"

The SOURCE-ORIGIN of Individual Self is the Consciousness Supreme – We are all different from each other in our physical body, mind and the intelligence, however, we have the same ATMIC SOURCE and WE ARE ALL ONE AT THE LEVEL OF BRAHMATMA.

The SOURCE-ORIGIN, the INFINITE SELF of the infinite number of Individual Selves is known as the Supra-Consciousness. The SOURCE-ORIGIN-INFINITE SELF is otherwise called as "BRAHMATMA" or "SARVA BHUTHATMA"or " Cosmic Self".

The greatest of all great truths states:
"Mamatma-Sarva-Bhuthatma"

"My Individual Self is The Cosmic Self Common To All Beings"

Victory is ever indicated by the THUMB.

The Supra-consciousness is represented by the 'THUMB'.

"BABA MUDRA"

The "BABA MUDRA" has the ring finger and middle finger held by the thumb. The two fingers not touched in BABA MUDRA are the little finger and the index finger.

The significance is that there is no need at all to tamper with the physical body in our spiritual endeavors! We should never trouble the physical body. Never!

The physical body is absolutely glorious and wonderful and is a pinnacle achievement of the Nature which is guided by the NATURE SPIRITS.

No need to practice difficult Hatha Yoga Kriyas!

No need of impossible Sheersha Asanas!

The second finger, the ring finger, that is Mind must be controlled, however. THE MIND must be thoroughly disciplined and should be totally rectified.

* * *

All the prejudices and stupidities of the SOCIETY are reflected truly in the INDIVIDUAL MIND. Such prejudices and stupidities of the Society hamper an individual's sanity and spiritual intelligence. Liquidating the impact of all the prejudices and stupidities of the Society on an individual's mind is the process of MEDITATION.

What can tame the Mind?

THE COSMIC SELF!

However, that should be 'agreed upon' by the Individual Self.

When the Individual Self wants to see that it is the mind that needs to be rectified and purified, it goes into MEDITATION. Then, the COSMIC SELF takes over, purifying and rectifying the Mind by means of its COSMIC ENERGY/COSMIC MIND.

This is the symbolic meaning of the RING FINGER being controlled by the THUMB FINGER in the "Baba Mudra".

* * *

Similarly, the limited INTELLIGENCE - BUDDHI, the MIDDLE FINGER, also needs to be tamed because the limited worldly INTELLIGENCE represents "half knowledge" and half Knowledge is absolutely dangerous.

* * *

HALF KNOWLEDGE is rectified only by FULL KNOWLEDGE and COSMIC SELF alone is FULL KNOWLEDGE.

This is the symbolic meaning of the MIDDLE FINGER being controlled by THUMB in the "Baba Mudra".

When the Individual Self 'decides' to become enlightened, it chooses to go into PRACTICE OF MEDITATION.

When the individual self chooses MEDITATION, then, the COSMIC SELF takes over and transforms the limited INTELLIGENCE that is the worldly INTELLIGENCE, with its spiritual Intelligence and spiritual Knowledge, which is also called as "SHUDDHA BUDDHI".

* * *

Transformation of "WORLDLY INTELLIGENCE" into "SPIRITUAL INTELLIGENCE", also is known as JNANA YOGA!

The most important thing to understand is that JNANA YOGA happens automatically and naturally while practicing DHYANA YOGA.

<u>Essence of "Baba Mudra"</u>

ring finger rectified = Dhyana Yoga

middle finger rectified = Jnana Yoga

Traveling from a state of "WORLDLY MIND" to a state of "SHUDDHA BUDDHI"…is called as MEDITATION or SPIRITUALITY or SPIRITUAL SCIENCE or ENLIGHTENMENT...

* * *

DO RIGHT MEDITATION

DO ANAPANASATI MEDITATION

BECOME A PERFECT MASTER

Brahmarshi Pithamaha Patriji,
Founder, Pyramid Spiritual Societies Movement,
India.

Pyramid Spiritual Societies Movement (PSSM) was founded by enlightened master Brahmarshi Pithamaha Patriji in the year 1990 with the objective of spreading the message of spiritual and harmonious living and bringing its benefits within the easy reach of all humanity, without any barriers of class, religion or region.

The Pyramid Spiritual Societies Movement is non-religious, non-cult, non-profit voluntary organization whose sole mission is to spread Anapanasati Meditation, Vegetarianism and Pyramid Power to one and all.

Brahmarshi Pithamaha Patriji 's approach has been scientific and secular and he has written over 70 books and traveled around the world, exploring and teaching universal truths to millions of spiritual seekers. Patriji has established over 10000 Pyramid Meditation centers around the globe with 20000 pyramids for Meditation.

www.pssmovement.org

MEETINGS THAT TRANSFORM!

By Sassanth

We are part of a single existence, a unified reality appearing distinct as spirit, mind and body. Meeting Pallavi was quite profound, like an important event that caused a change of direction in my life. Truly it is impossible for life to be as we know it, if this reality was divided.

My meeting with Pallavi happened through a spiritual group we are in. One day I posted a random comment to a post and it felt like the words came from deep thought, this led to a discussion and that discussion went on, we started to talk from that point, and it never stopped. The discussions would always be of the truest spiritual nature.

To me connecting with my inner being had been quite accidental which led me to have a strange life, because I could never find out why I was the way I am. The divided world felt lonely, but, after meeting Pallavi I realized 'in this day and age extraordinary people live amongst us', and it is within us all. During our various discussions she shared vivid visions of the worlds she had been to in her meditation. I listened without uttering a word because she was actually describing what I had seen myself, and the details were always exact, but I never could tell her that, 'she was sharing with me beliefs I carried within me all my life, and she always wanted me to go higher'. Through her I was actually confirming all is One. I realized she could make connections at a soul level. I really wished for her to share her knowledge and experiences with the world because a person like her understands the science of within through practice and who did this while also being a successful individual at all facets of life.

When she told me about the book she was writing about Babaji, I was ecstatic. I wanted to see the work completed. Today as I read these words in the book I will confirm to you, we are GOD, for we all are in GOD and from GOD and our destination is GOD.

Like the great sage Vivekananda quoted 'As the different streams having their sources in different places all mingle their water in the sea, O Lord, the different paths which men take through different tendencies varies though they appear crooked or straight, all lead to Thee' (Siva Mahimam Stotram 7).

Pallavi connects us to our real nature, the real nature of the thinking and knowing human being, this book will validate you, like her words and experiences have validated me to go deeper and within us there are treasures greater than anything we have ever imagined.

This book will open a new chapter in the consciousness of humanity. With these words, a new dimension of presenting one's truth, a scientific observation of the within, will become part of our consciousness. Written with the flow of words so elegant, you will feel you are observing the conversation first hand. This book will connect you to Babaji, the great master who reaches us all without our knowing. Now the time has come to know.

Sassanth M Shanmadhuran,
CEO and Founder,
Stellar Innovations Group,
Qatar.

ABOUT THE AUTHOR

Master Pallavi is an ardent meditation expert. She is a Senior Pyramid Master working dedicatedly for Pyramid Spiritual Societies Movement from the past 14 years.

Her life transformed after practicing Anapanasati Meditation. She continues to spread the science of spirituality by taking seasoned workshops.

Throughout her journey, she has embraced skills like clairvoyance but under the right guidance of her Guru Brahmarshi Pitamaha Patriji, she could truly understand it's purpose.

A change-maker by spirit, she is Founder and Director at Mad buddhas. It serves as a platform and doorway for all artists, writers alike who wish to create products to spread the science of spirituality throughout the world. The company has released animation shorts on vegetarianism, the importance of meditation and mindfulness.

GLOSSARY

Ahamkara	-	Ego
Anapanasati	-	Meditation done by observance of breath
Angvastram	-	Cloth worn to cover shoulders
Atma	-	Soul
Atma Lokam	-	World of Souls
Baba Mudra	-	A type of symbol of fingers in Hatha Yoga propounded by Mahavatar Babaji
Brahmarshi	-	A rishi who has become one with Brahman
Brahmatma	-	Original Creative Energy/ Consciousness
Deep	-	Lamp
Dhyanam	-	Meditation
Dhyanasadhana	-	Practice of Meditation
Dhyana Yoga	-	Yoga of meditation

Dhoti	-	Apparel worn by Hindu males
Gita	-	Bhagavad-Gita, the most sacred scripture of Hindus
Hatha Yoga	-	The yoga of physical perfection
Jata	-	Matted hair
Jeevatma	-	The individual soul/ consciousness
Jnana Yoga	-	Yoga of knowledge/wisdom
Jyoti	-	Light
Kailas	-	A sacred peak in Himalayas
Kanthi Lokam	-	Light World
Karma	-	Action operating through the Law of Cause & Effect
Kriya Yoga	-	Hatha Yogic exercise
Mahadev	-	Name for Lord Shiva, the Hindu God
Mahavatar Babaji	-	Guru from the Himalayas or Exalted Master
Mahayogi	-	Exalted Spiritual Master

Mamatma-Sarva-Bhuthatma	-	One Self
Pithamaha	-	Father figure in the lineage of Spiritual Gurus
Pyramid Energies	-	Energy that is available from pyramids
Pyramid Master	-	One who utilizes energy of pyramids to meditate
Sadhna	-	Meditational practice
Sangha	-	A group of enlightened souls
Sanyasi	-	Renunciate, monk
Samadhi	-	The state of super consciousness where Absoluteness is experienced
Sarva Bhutatma	-	Energy that pervades every being including elementals
Satya Lokam	-	World where only Truth prevails, highest dimension
Sattvik	-	Pure
Shastrartha	-	True Meaning of scriptures
Sheersha Asanas	-	Head below, legs up pose in yogic exercise

Shiva	- Deity revered as 'The Absolute'
Shuddha Buddhi	- Pure intelligence
Sajjan-sangatya	- Company of self-realized, like-minded people
Siddhis	- Major psychic powers; perfections
Sutras	- A rule or aphorism in Sanskrit literature
Tamil Nadu	- Province in Southern India
Upanishads	- Vedic literature
Vasuki	- Name of snake that is referred in Hindu Mythology
Vedas	- The revealed scripture of the Hindus containing the Upanishads
Yogi	- One who practices Yoga